Barbers

Three Hundred Years of a Farming Family

- V C Boothman -

Published by

AJ & RG Barber Limited
Maryland Farm,
Ditcheat, Shepton Mallet
Somerset BA4 6PR

© 2012 Valerie Boothman

ISBN 978-0-9574254-0-8

FIRST EDITION

Contents

A J Barber

R G Barber

Introduction

Val Boothman had been retired for nine years when Charlie and I approached her in our village pub, The Manor Inn, Ditcheat and asked her to write the story of AJ and RG Barber. For some time we had been discussing that a book should be written so that all the anecdotes and stories we had heard in our youth would not be lost. We had in fact had meetings with possible authors but were not convinced that they would write the story in the style we had in mind. We had a further meeting with Val when she agreed but suggested that she would start with the history of the family which would lead into the history of the company.

Val joined the company in 1972 having returned to England with her family from a five year period in Zambia. In those days our family business was growing but the buildings were old and there was a need for much investment. Looking back it seems there was never a time of consolidation. Adjoining farms would come on the market and finances would be stretched to purchase them. As sales of cheese increased the dairy capacity had to be increased, automation introduced, more offices built, cold stores erected, staff to interview and train, customers to court, and decisions to be taken. The story had to be written. In this story Val has managed to give the reader a comprehensive history of farming life in Somerset which we gladly feel will interest a wider audience than our original intention.

Giles Barber

Preface

The ceremonial and non-metropolitan County of Somerset in South West England borders Bristol and South Gloucestershire to the north, Wiltshire to the east, Dorset to the south-east and Devon to the south-west. It is partly bounded to the north and west by the Bristol Channel and the estuary of the River Severn. The City of Bath has returned to Somerset but the county town is Taunton in the south. Somerset is a rural county of rolling hills such as the Blackdown Hills, Mendip Hills, Quantock Hills and Exmoor National Park with large flat expanses of land including the Somerset Levels. There is evidence of human occupation from Palaeolithic times and of subsequent settlement in the Roman and Anglo-Saxon periods. The County played a significant part in the consolidation of power and rise of King Alfred the Great and later in the English Civil War and the Monmouth Rebellion.

Apple orchards were once plentiful and Somerset is still known for the production of strong Cider. Agriculture is a major business in the County, farming of sheep, cattle and pigs and the production of the famous West Country Farmhouse Cheddar. It is believed that when Cheddar cheese was developed by the villagers of Cheddar, Somerset with its rich pastures, was considered the centre of England's dairy industry. According to a local tale, a milk-maid kept a bucket full of milk in the Cheddar caves. She forgot to collect it and at a later stage found that the milk had transformed into something else, which tasted good. This incident prompted the villagers to try to develop the product.

It is not proved whether the Cheddar cheese made at that time carried any resemblance to the present day cheddar. Later, a local system was developed to make cheddar cheese, by collecting milk from livestock farmers. Each farmer received his share in proportion to the quantity of milk contributed by him.

Though there is no evidence to prove the exact time of invention of cheddar it is said that the official accounts of King Henry II (1154-1189) mention the purchase of 10,000 pounds of cheddar cheese. So this cheese can be dated back to the late 12th century. How King Henry purchased such a large amount is a mystery. Perhaps an extra zero was added in error. At that time the cheese was made by the dairy farmers and there is no record of mass production. In the 17th, 18th and 19th centuries cheese along with cider was produced on the farms for consumption by their families and as part payment for labour to agricultural workers.

This is the story of a farming family starting with John Barber born in 1712. The story includes the history and current position of the manufacture of West Country Farmhouse Cheddar. It contains anecdotes, records of residence and records of a successful and expanding family business, details of which would be lost if not preserved.

In my research many people have been kind enough to help and their assistance is noted in the acknowledgements. I have endeavoured to ensure that the facts I have written are all true but I apologise should there be errors.

Valerie Boothman - Author

The Ancestors

This story of a West Country farming family spans three hundred years. The earliest records are of John Barber born in 1712 in the village of West Lydford, Somerset. John married Joan Porch of West Pennard in Wells in 1735. They had six children; Mary (died in infancy), William, another Mary, James, John and Thomas. John's second son James Barber was born in 1741 and married Grace Duke in 1765 and after her death married Elizabeth Welchman in 1774. James had five children; William, Elizabeth, James, Alice, and Grace.

William, the eldest son, was born in 1770 in West Lydford and was a yeoman. His mother died when he was aged four years. In 1794 he married Elizabeth March and they had nine children, the last being Daniel Barber who was born in 1810. When Elizabeth died in 1826 William married a widow Ann Davis. When he died in 1842 aged seventy-two only his daughter Jane and son Daniel had survived him. This sad situation ironically benefited Daniel financially.

Yeomanry:

In Britain, Yeomanry, a volunteer cavalry force, organised in 1761 for home defence which merged into the Territorial Army in 1907. A Yeoman was a man holding and cultivating a small landed estate; a freeholder, a person qualified for certain duties and rights, such as to serve on juries and vote for the knight of the shire, by virtue of possessing free land of an annual income of 40 shillings.

(Oxford Dictionaries Online)

When Daniel inherited his father's wealth in 1843 he was able to purchase Maryland Farm. His father's Will stated that daughter Jane must be allowed to "dwell in the house in Ditcheat". Had the other seven siblings been alive and shared the estate, Daniels circumstances would have been very different.

Daniel had married Rebecca Reakes in 1835 in St Mary Magdalene Church in Ditcheat. The 1841 census shows Daniel and his family living at Maryland Farm as a tenant farmer, farming a few acres and employing agricultural labourers. They milked cows, made cheese, and farmed pigs.

Ditcheat is a small village although St Mary Magdalene Church (known to have 12th century origins) and the Priory or Abbey where the Rectors of Ditcheat resided was historically linked to Glastonbury Abbey, 12 miles away. The Priory was built in the early 15th century and a plaque on the wall of the church shows the first Rector of Ditcheat lived there in 1425. Documentation shows that monks were housed where Abbey Farm now stands whilst the Priory was being built. The chapel was part of the original building and the room below was known as "the withdraw".

These monks were travellers in so far as they regularly travelled from London to Glastonbury and would probably have stayed in Ditcheat on their way to Southampton where they would leave for Europe. In the Doomsday book of 1086 Ditcheat belonged to Glastonbury Abbey and contained 36 families. In 2012 it has a population of approximately 750. The fact that Ditcheat has not ballooned into a major town is why it is to this day an attractive village.

In the 1830's and 40's while Daniel was living at Maryland Farm it was a time when railways and canals were being built throughout England to carry produce to and from the ports to towns and cities. Dairy farmers who made cheese farmed pigs as a way of disposing of the whey which was fed to the pigs. Pigs were fattened at Maryland Farm until 1990 when the pig units were demolished.

The Enterprising West Country Farmers

In the early 1840's life was difficult for small farmers in Somerset, as in other parts of the country. One subject which very much concerned Daniel and his farming neighbours during the severe agricultural depression was the price they were receiving for their produce from the London dealers in Newgate Market and Smithfield.

These farmers frequented The Market Inn in Shepton Mallet, six miles from Ditcheat where one Saturday evening in 1844 a very special meeting took place. They talked into the early hours and helped no doubt by the amount of refreshment they consumed decided that something had to be done. The decision was made to send one of them to London to deal directly with the market buyers. It would have to be someone they could trust, preferably a farmer, a man of energy and enterprise. It was not possible for Daniel to go, his father had died in 1842 and by then his brothers had died too so he could not leave Ditcheat. The man the farmers chose to entrust with their produce was William Lovell who farmed near Glastonbury. He was then aged 54, a mature, responsible man of integrity.

A few Sundays later he climbed on board the mail coach armed with a list of cheese, butter, pork and beef being offered by the farmers who supported the plan. That night he arrived at The Cross Keys Inn, St John Street, Smithfield. Although weary from his journey, he rose early next morning and proceeded on foot visiting retailers in and about the City. By the end of the week William Lovell had sold all the goods on his list, proving that his friends had chosen wisely in trusting him to represent them. On Saturday he paid his bill at The Cross Keys and took the coach back to Shepton Mallet.

There were more than a few jugs of ale and cider consumed in the bar parlour of the Market Inn that night. So pleased were the farmers with the prices William had obtained for them that they decided that he should continue this venture on a regular basis. They undertook to help his wife Mary to run the farm near Glastonbury during his absences. The arrangement worked well for four years until William decided to sell his farm and move his family to London where he could devote his time fully to the new business. The day the family left Somerset for London it was raining hard and the three sons had to sit outside the coach. It became so wet that the boys were actually sitting in pools of water.

When the coach stopped for the horses to be changed one of the brothers jumped down from the coach and bought a grid iron to sit on. The family moved into rooms above a tobacconists shop but later moved to Snow Hill where William remained until his death in 1864. The business flourished and the West Country connection became stronger by the injection of fresh capital from relatives in Somerset. They acquired new offices by purchasing The Cross Keys Inn where William had stayed on his first visit to London. By the turn of the century, from being agents for West Country farmers they had become food importers on a massive scale.

To return to the original story, Daniel too was delighted by the prices he was now receiving for all his hard work. Profits were used to expand his farm and facilities. The 1851 census shows Daniel and his family living at Maryland although it was then listed as "Merry Lands" and he was then a farmer of 73 acres employing four labourers. Living with Daniel and wife Rebecca were their sons Alfred aged fourteen, Joseph aged thirteen, Thomas aged eight, lodger William Reakes (Daniel's brother in law) and servant Mary Baby aged twelve.

Sadly Daniel died of "consumption" (tuberculosis) in 1853 aged 42. His eldest son Alfred may have gone to America according to family stories and certainly the New York Passenger lists 1820-1957 show an Alfred Barber making several return journeys from Liverpool to New York. Daniel's son Joseph died aged twenty in 1859 but fortunately his youngest son Thomas continued the dairy and pig farming business. At the time of Daniel's death in 1853 the countryside was changing.

In 1853 the population of mainland UK had risen to 21 million with 2.3 million people living in London. For the first time in history more people in Britain lived in towns than in the countryside. The population living in towns was growing at an increasing rate and Britain was now unique in the world being essentially an urban nation. The industrial revolution transformed the landscape. Railways, canals, new roads and improving transport infrastructure provided fresh food for fast growing towns while imported produce from around the world provided a greatly more diverse diet. Produce which had been sent by stagecoach had taken days to arrive and now by rail it took only hours. Increasingly however, the countryside became a remote and distant environment to an industrialised society. Capital spending on drainage, buildings, machinery and roads linking to the railways all fuelled the agricultural revolution with British farmers at least twice as efficient as their European contemporaries. In 1860 80% of food consumed was produced in the UK but by the 1870's after a series of bad harvests and the arrival of imports, farm gate prices fell dramatically and the great agricultural depression ensued.

What was happening in the rest of the world at this time? America had just purchased California and New Mexico from Mexico for $15 million following the American/Mexico war (1846 – 1848) and there was growing unrest resulting in the American Civil War 1860-1866. In 1867 America went on to purchase Alaska (586,412 square miles) from Russia at a cost of $7.2 million a mere two cents per acre. Nevertheless these were difficult times but not everyone was suffering. When the Earl of Yarborough died in 1875, his stock of cigars was sold for £850, the equivalent of 18 years' pay for the impoverished labourers on his estate.

These were not easy times for Daniel's son Thomas to take over the reins. The 1881 census shows Thomas and family living in Rectory Farm, which was later named Abbey Farm, a farmhouse only fifty yards from Maryland Farm and cheese was also made there.

Rectory Farmhouse is a square solid grey stone house situated across the paddock from The Priory whereas Maryland Farm house was a more modest cottage. Ten years later Thomas and his family lived at Highbridge Farm on the outskirts of Ditcheat. In the 1890's Thomas and his son Alfred were ahead of their times by introducing horse drawn machinery for haymaking.

There was a tragedy in the family in 1897. Thomas's youngest son and fifth child, Daniel James Barber, was aged 22 and lived with one of his sisters at Bengrove Farm on the Fosse Way (Roman Road) just outside Ditcheat. It was reported in The Bristol Times and Mirror of June 1897 of a death by suicide. On the 3rd of June Daniel James Barber had purchased "sixpenny-worth" (2 oz) of arsenic from a chemist in the nearest town, Shepton Mallet, to use on the farm. After dinner with his sister he had left the farm to go for a walk but when he did not return she had called her father. He found Daniel lying unconscious under a hedge where he died shortly afterwards. Dr Coombs of Castle Cary said he had been treating Daniel James for depression for five years. At this time Daniel James' elder brother Alfred Gerald was aged 25 and involved in farming with his father Thomas.

By 1901 Thomas was a successful farmer and more cheese was being made and more land acquired. He moved to live in Prospect House, a rather grand house, on the edge of the village overlooking the fields of Maryland Farm. His eldest son Alfred moved into Rectory Farm with his new wife Mary Elizabeth, known in the family as Polly, and eventually known as Granny Barber. The 1911 census lists daughter Mary age 6 and son Thomas age 3. Alfred John (Jack) and Reginald Gerald were yet to be born. On the day that Gerald was born his Mother Polly gave birth to him in the morning and was reputedly up and making cheese before the day was out.

The census shows her occupation as "assisting husband" but in actual fact apart from running the farmhouse and bearing children she was a skilled cheese maker. She was a very hard working farmer's wife with an astute brain. Alfred was a very good farmer who also enjoyed reading and was more academic than Polly. He was very much involved with the church and was the Church Warden for many years. He was also a very generous man and had a reputation for helping anyone in the village who had come on hard times. Many years later their daughter Mary told her niece Anna that her mother would jokingly say "Alfred, I make the money and you give it away".

In the years before the war the eldest child Mary helped her mother to make cheese and the sons, Thomas, Alfred John (Jack) and Reginald Gerald (known as Gerald) all helped on the farm. Thomas (also known as Farmer Tom) was later to leave home and set up his own farm and separate commercial cheesemaking dairy but the two brothers Jack and Gerald were destined to work together and establish a business which would in time be registered as AJ & RG Barber Limited.

The Early 1900's

In the early 1900's the family business was growing. In 1920 the Leirs who owned not only The Priory, but Abbey Farm, outbuildings, and a considerable acreage of land in and around Ditcheat were advised by their brokers to sell most of the land and to invest in war bonds. War bonds were debt securities issued by a government for the purpose of financing military operations during the war. Pressure to buy war bonds was often accompanied with appeals to patriotism and conscience.

Nevertheless many local tenant farmers now had to purchase the land they farmed and had no choice but to finance the purchase from the Leirs. Alfred Barber paid £100 an acre for a hundred acres which adjoined Maryland Farm but the Barber family were allowed to continue to pay a rent for Abbey Farm, the outbuildings and sixty acres. In those days this would have seemed a considerable amount of money and for the next twelve years Alfred could do no more than break even on the farm. In spite of having to purchase the land he managed to educate his four children privately.

Eventually the farmhouse at Maryland was converted into a store, later an engineering workshop and the farm buildings adjoining the old farmhouse were converted into a cheese making dairy. There is a water colour painting of the farmhouse in it's hey day when it was a lovely old building with chickens running around in the front garden. This water colour painting was used when the company decided to market Maryland Farmhouse Mature

Cheddar under its own label. In later years the dairy had to be extended numerous times; offices were built, cold stores and milk silos erected. During one of the building programmes at Maryland Farm, the builders discovered a carving on one of the old oak beams. It just said 1833. The family were aware that cheese had been made on the premises as far back as 1833 and it sounded a good name for a cheese. The carving is there to this day in the Directors Office.

There is a family story told about a time in the early 1900's when Alfred Barber imported a revolutionary grass mowing machine from the United States of America. This was the first machine of its kind in Ditcheat and probably the County. It was a huge event at the time and it is probable that his Uncle, Alfred Barber (born 1837) who had gone to America in his youth, was involved in this import. Until this machine arrived on the farm the grass was cut by lines of farm workers using scythes and rakes. This system was very labour intensive. When the horse drawn mowing machine arrived, to the consternation of the farm workers, the grass was cut and shaped into neat rows. The workers saw this as a threat to their livelihood and one night under darkness they crept out into the field which was to be mowed the next day and buried pieces of metal in the ground to foul the blades. Of course this act of sabotage did not delay labour saving machinery being introduced into farming but it is yet another example of how man will react to progress when his livelihood is at stake.

During one of Alfred Barbers (born 1837) visits home he brought two beautiful blue "Closonie" vases. They were very well packaged to protect them from the journey. They are quite stunning and have been passed down through the generations and Christopher Barber was delighted to receive them from his Aunt Anna.

During both World Wars farmers were responsible for producing food for the nation and many were exempt from joining the Armed Forces but joined the Home Guard. In World War II farmers produce was sent to a central distribution depot. This was a system known as "War Ag" whereby the Government instructed farmers which crops they should grow. Before the war many farmers had struggled to make a living getting very poor returns for their efforts. Milk was sold at a shilling (five new pence) a gallon. Consequently farmers appreciated the better prices they received during the war when food was rationed and imports were reduced due to supply lines being severely hampered by enemy action.

In the 1930's Wards Farm on the outskirts of Ditcheat was purchased from a Mr Francis Clark (there is now no record of the price paid) by Jack and Gerald Barber. With the purchase was an agreement with the manager of Prideaux Milk Factory in Evercreech that 6d a gallon would be paid for the milk produced at Wards Farm. The contract was dishonoured and they were only paid 4d per gallon. This was a huge reduction in the price that had been agreed and anticipated and was a bitter blow at the time.

Alfred and Mary moved to Park House on the edge of Ditcheat leaving Gerald and his family in Rectory Farm the name had now been changed to Abbey Farm. Alfred Barber died in 1949 and his wife Mary (Polly), stayed with her children for three month periods at a time until her death. Farmer Tom married Helen

Look from Ditcheat and they lived at Brue Farm, Lovington, Somerset. He purchased cheesemaking equipment from the previous owners of the farm and started making cheese. Jack Barber lived in Manor Farm on the edge of Ditcheat, a farm he purchased in 1939, the very day war was declared. The land at Manor Farm was purchased from George Dyke at £30 an acre. Jack married Margery Weeks in 1940 and it was there they brought up their three children Richard, Paul and Anna. After Margery died in 1947 Jack married Daphne Hoadley and her daughter Sandra was also brought up at Manor Farm Ditcheat.

Gerald married Dorothy Steel Noel and they lived in Abbey Farm with their children Patricia, Nicholas and Gillian. Dorothy loved to play tennis and held tennis parties at Abbey Farm quite frequently. Gerald had a love of boats which was passed down to Nicky who in later years had his own yacht and took part in the Fastnet, the Round Britain Yacht Race and the two handed race to Iceland. Gerald also hunted regularly and both Nicky and Gill joined him as active members of the Blackmore Vale and Sparkford Hunt.

The Next Generation

Jack's sons Paul and Richard showed entrepreneurial skills as teenagers by taking orders for parcels of cheese whilst at school and delivering the cheese on their bikes on a Monday morning. On one occasion the School Chaplain ordered some cheese and gave it to his sister who was visiting from London. She happened to work for Sainsbury's Head Office and gave it to her boss who liked it so much he contacted the company and so began a long relationship with the Supermarket.

Richard had shown huge interest in farming from a very early age and wished to be independent so at the age of only seventeen his father took out a bank loan and bought him his own farm at Seaborough in Dorset. It is probable that his father kept a close eye on the development for a few years. The children had been brought up to work hard and from an early age had responsibilities. Paul was an excellent cricketer but as he grew up knew that his career would be in the family farming business.

The business was expanding and when Paul left school he continued to help his father manage the farms as he had done during school holidays. This meant rising at 5 am to milk the cows and then do a good days work. It was inevitable that gradually Paul would take over farm management from his father.

As he played less and less cricket locally Paul showed great interest in Somerset County Cricket and although he too supported the local hunt his passion for National Hunt Horse

Racing was developing. He has been a director of Taunton Race Course for many years. He was still quite young when his dream was to milk 1000 cows and own a horse which would win The Cheltenham Gold Cup.

All Jack and Gerald's children spent their formative years involved in the business. A huge number of cheese miniatures were sold especially at Christmas and their young knuckles were sore handling them. The Cheddar and Caerphilly miniatures were made individually, about a pound in weight and were dipped in hot wax. It was always impossible to produce enough for the Christmas orders so again the family members who farmed and made cheese in the locality made miniatures to try to meet the demand.

Gerald's daughter Gill tells of an occasion when she had to deliver some cheese to Bristol. When she arrived it was lunch time and the loading bay staff were having their break so she decided to off load the cheese herself. Suddenly there was uproar as the men appeared and challenged her because she was not a member of their Union. Gill thought quickly and said "Well I am a fully paid up member of the NFU" (The National Farmers Union) and although they were rather confused they allowed her to continue off loading the cheese and they went back to their lunch break.

The cheese making skills had been passed down from Granny Barber to Edgar Hodges who lived in the village and when Nicholas left school he worked for another farmer to gain cheese making and management skills and then worked with Edgar to gain further knowledge. Edgar remained with the company for over forty years by which time Nicholas was in full control of cheese making and management of the dairy. The company enjoyed benefiting from the advice given to them by Kay Maddever when making Territorial Cheeses. This professional and qualified lady was famous for helping all the Farmhouse Cheesemakers. In later years George Fowler the Unigate Territorial Cheesemaker had retired and visited Ditcheat once a week to assist the Company.

St. Peters Church, Lydford on Fosse

Built in 1844 on the site of the old church where John Barber married Joan Porch in 1735

Flossie Penny packing Caerphilly wheels

Proud driver Bill Meader with his new delivery truck. C. 1958

Haymaking at Maryland Farm. C. 1948

Jack Barber c. 1952

Diane Duncan, Jack Barber, Gerald Barber, Dorothy Barber (nee Noel), Betty Bates, Mary Martin. Cardiff July 1939.

Jack, Gerald and Mary Barber c. 1920

Haymaking at Maryland Farm c. 1920

Alfred Barber with young son Jack

Jack Jones with Horse and Wagon at Abbey Farm c. 1920

Mary, Thomas, Jack, Gerald, Alfred & Polly Barber c. 1918

Thomas Barber & family in front of Prospect House, Ditcheat c.1914

Thomas Barber & family in front of Prospect House, Ditcheat c.1914

Dorothy, Gill, Gerald, Nicky, Tricia (with Shotty and Tweetie) c.1950

Gerald Barber c.1965

N.F.U. President Lord Henry Plum visits Maryland Farm in 1971

Dairy Produce Packers sales convention held at Abey Farm, Ditcheat in 1973
DPP Staff and members of the Barber families

Jack Barber and Val Boothman 1975

Church of Saint Mary Magdalene, Ditcheat

Making Caerphilly Commercially and Widening The Customer Base

It would be approximately 1952 when Gerald Barber took his wife Dorothy to Cardiff to visit relatives in the town. They were sitting having tea and Gerald was rather bored with the conversation so excused himself and went across the road to the Co-operative Wholesale Society Store to look at the prices they were charging for cheese. He noticed the quantity of Caerphilly being sold and also the selling price. He knew that Caerphilly could be sold within a month of manufacture so the cheese maker would very quickly have a return for the cost of the milk. He spoke to the buyer who suggested he brought a sample for him to see the next time he was in Cardiff. Gerald explained that he could not make just one cheese, it would have to be a whole day's make, about eighty 9 lb wheels. The buyer decided to take a chance and a deal was struck.

A month later when Gerald arrived in his old truck with the "wheels" of Caerphilly cheese carefully lying on sweet hay and covered by a linen cloth, he was astounded. Gerald explained he had no packing material so they stacked the cheeses into egg boxes to be carried into the store. The Coal Miners of South

Wales preferred to take Caerphilly cheese in their sandwiches as other fillings such as meat would sweat underground. They enjoyed the salty acidity of Caerphilly and of course it had been made in small quantities on local farms in the valleys for years. The Caerphilly cheese could be made one day and cheddar cheese made the next day depending on the demand.

The demand for Caerphilly Cheese grew and the wheels were also made at Brue Farm (Uncle Tom) and by the Longmans at Bagborough (Auntie Mary) but marketed by the company. The cheese was placed in brine, then dusted in whitening and rice flour to develop a slight rind and placed on shelves before despatching. Until the coal mines closed in the 1970's Barbers enjoyed good business selling Caerphilly cheese to South Wales while always continuing cheddar production.

During the 1950's and 60's Gerald worked hard at expanding sales and manned stands at The London Dairy Show in Olympia, previously known as the Royal International Dairy Show. The show had been held at Olympia since 1876 and was considered to be the highlight of the UK's farming calendar. It covered a wide range of breeds, produce, poultry and cheese. The family were also there to support him and they were competing with many other cheese makers to broaden their customer base.

It was on one of these occasions that Gerald secured the business to supply Whitelocks in Stockton on Tees in north east England. As he completed the agreement he was aware it would entail purchasing a second lorry! Gerald instilled in his family much enthusiasm for supporting the Dairy Show and customers were regularly entertained on the stand. When the show moved to Stoneleigh in Warwickshire in 1974 he was convinced that their presence at Olympia had served its purpose.

The "Limited Company"

In 1955 the brothers Jack and Gerald (AJ & RG) decided that the business needed to expand and be placed on a more commercial basis. The site at Maryland Farm required investment. They had the foresight to see that the company could be more than a small family farming business. More land should be purchased, fields to be stocked but the main objective was to increase the cheese making capacity in the dairy at Maryland Farm. The decision was made to visit the Bank Manager in Shepton Mallet and armed with their business plan they attended a meeting. That evening they celebrated a loan of £100,000. The business was then registered as a limited company and Barbers became AJ & RG Barber Limited. Later a second company was registered AJ & RG Barber (Sales) Limited who would purchase all the production from the main company and be responsible for selling it. However in the course of time they also purchased cheese from other cheese makers and sold it under different brand names

As cheese sales increased, more land was purchased, more fields were stocked and more milk produced for cheesemaking. When the company acquired *"The Meadow"* milking unit and the land in 1964 it needed considerable investment. A large overdraft with the bank was necessary to pay for a modern herring-bone milking system and winter facilities for the cattle. Until then the cows were tethered during winter months in simple cow sheds. In 1968 the land for *"Eastontrow"* milking unit was purchased from Dick Longman who retained the farmhouse in Alhampton and he remained good friends especially with Paul, until his death.

In about 1967 more land was purchased from the Golledge family adjoining Dairy Farm House at Lower Wraxall just outside Ditcheat. The actual farmhouse was not required and was sold to Francis Sutton. Frank had worked as a Sales Representative for Avery's Wine in Bristol but was looking for employment and fortuitously Barbers needed an office manager. Frank joined the company and worked until his retirement at the age of seventy. He had a wry sense of humour and was known to comment "the tyranny of the fortunate" if he considered any person of wealth had exploited their position.

The families at Manor Farm and Abbey Farm were growing so Jack and Daphne moved to a new bungalow "The Oaks" on the edge of the village leaving Paul and his family to live at Manor Farm. Gerald and Dorothy remained at Abbey Farm until their deaths at which time Nicky and his family moved there.

Family Anecdotes

Most of the employees were and are drawn from the village and there are some lovely stories. Nicholas tells of an evening when he decided to ensure that all was well in the dairy and he heard a noise from an area on a mezzanine floor where cheese cloths were stored. He thought it was a rat or something and decided to check. As he quietly climbed the ladder he could see in the darkness the figure of one of his cheese makers in an embarrassing position with one of the girl workers. When they saw him they were horrified but he quickly apologised for interrupting them and descended the ladder.

Alfred John Barber was always known locally and addressed as "Farmer Jack". His younger brother Reginald Gerald was similarly addressed as "Farmer Gerald". Only visitors addressed them as Mr Barber. Their sons were known as, and addressed as, Paul and Nicky. In the 1960's cheese was being delivered to customers in London, Manchester, South Wales, Welwyn Garden City, and Stockton-on-Tees. Barbers had one second hand lorry and in the days before motorways and modern equipment it was a long 700 mile round trip to Stockton-on-Tees, so a second lorry was purchased.

Another family story is about the day when the driver 'phoned in to say he was very ill and could not do the trip to the North East that day. Gerald lost no time in telling Nicky he would have to deliver the cheese as "you never disappoint the customer". At the end of a long drive, Nicky was pleased to see the customer's premises and a large giant of a man was there to meet him and direct him where to park the lorry. As Nicky jumped down from the cab the man aggressively approached him. "So are you Barber's driver?" Nicky answered "Well, yes I suppose I am". With that the man challenged Nicky and said "So you are the chap who has got my daughter into trouble are you?" It took some minutes for Nicky to realise why his driver had "taken sick" that day and to explain who he really was.

This wasn't the only time Nicky had driven the lorry. His father did not suffer fools gladly and when an employee offended for some misdemeanour Nicky would plead with his father not to sack the man as it was usually Nicky who had to pick up the pieces and temporarily replace him. He well remembers the first ever occasion he drove the lorry a long distance which involved an over night stop. Bed and breakfast would be at a transport café which had accommodation for the drivers and their vehicles.

The small narrow beds were several to a room and Nicky noticed that he was the only "lorry driver" who changed into pyjamas before getting into bed. He was not the only one who noticed it as there were quite a few muffled giggles, and even more so when he took his toilet bag along to the hand basin to wash and clean his teeth. On his first night a man in the next bed pointed to Nicky's boots he had placed close by "are you intending wearing those tomorrow?" he asked. "Well of course" said Nicky. "Then if I were you I would put a leg of your bed in each boot as we do and then they may still be here in the morning" he said.

Sure enough as Nicky looked at the other beds the other lorry drivers had done the same. During the night as he looked along the line of beds he could see the lit ends of cigarettes, tiny red glows in the darkness. Something else he had to get used to was the noises from each bed during the night. It was all pretty basic. This young man was in a world to which he was unaccustomed.

In the 50's, 60's, and 70's, the cheese delivered to towns and cities in December would also carry gifts of holly from the hedgerows and mistletoe from the Somerset apple orchards which Paul and Nicky had collected. This was very popular with the customers receiving the cheese. In particular the staff of Dairy Produce Packers in Plumstead, London, would make sure they were around when the Barbers lorry arrived.

The Milk Marketing Board

No story of a dairy farming family business would be complete without mentioning the MMB. The Milk Marketing Board for England and Wales, established in 1933, was certainly the greatest commercial enterprise ever launched by British farmers. In terms of its main activity – the collection and sale of milk from farms – it was the largest such organisation in the world.

At its peak it marketed annually 13,000 million litres of milk, twice that of its nearest rival in the USA. The Milk Marketing scheme lasted just over 60 years being revoked in November 1994. Milk, of all agricultural products, is the most difficult to market. It is liquid, heavy, and the most awkward to transport. It is also as "nature's finest food" a first class medium for bacterial growth and highly perishable. Additionally it is produced in family farming units with, usually, either big buyers to contend with or uncertain distant markets to face.

Attempts at harnessing producer power in the early part of the twentieth century did not prove sufficient to withstand the instability of the market. Therefore originating out of a producer need in the 1930's the Board was created by the government. It was in this context of a difficult product to sell in a buyer dominated and unstable market that the Board had its origin. It was a government agency established to control milk production and distribution. It functioned as a buyer of 'last resort' in the British milk market, thereby guaranteeing a minimum price for milk producers.

Most countries relied on government regulated import control but the UK had, and still has, a high dependence on imports. The British dairy farmers were thus provided with an alternative in milk marketing schemes that strengthened their negotiating position and had a pricing system that safely secured the liquid market away from the unstable influence of supplies sold for manufacture of cheese and dairy products.

The dissolution in 1994 had many critics but by then pressures were mounting that made the MMB unsustainable. The EU had mounted a number of legal challenges against the end use pricing system that operated at the time. The existence of state owned market boards sat uncomfortably with the Conservative government's free market philosophy. The pressure bearing down on the MMB was so great that it had no option but to consider proposals that would bring about its eventual demise.

When the MMB was revoked in 1994 a large single co-operative was created called Milk Marque. As a near monopoly supplier of milk the MMB had had huge power in the marketplace, inviting processors to bid for volumes of milk at predetermined prices. With no independent arbitrator, farmgate prices now rocketed, topping 25p per litre in 1996, threatening the viability of processors. The whole system came under attack on 'competition grounds'. Processors challenged Milk Marque on ten allegations of distorting competition. They were found guilty on nine of them. The upshot was that in 2000 Milk Marque was split into three regional co-operatives; they engaged in mergers to increase their scale and embarked on a series of acquisitions to develop processing capacity. Major dairies also expanded and rationalised to boost their efficiency. Many critics think that the old marketing scheme gave producers and processors a guaranteed margin. They did not have to think about efficiency, customer service, or product development.

The rest of the world was investing for the future where a real market existed. Now the whole milk market is more transparent and there is a greater emphasis on efficiency – both among farmers and processors. In 2002 The Milk Group merged with Zenith to form Dairy Farmers of Britain. Unfortunately this business went into receivership in 2009.

Barbers were no longer restricted by milk quotas. They had always used milk from their own herds for cheese production and they bought milk from other West Country farmers but their purchase of this milk was controlled by the MMB. Even the manufacture of cheese was regulated under quotas and Barbers were restricted as to how much Cheddar cheese they could make.

In the late 1990's Barbers realised the way forward was for them to purchase milk direct from milk producers. Farmers were courted and offered contracts to supply their milk at a fixed price for a fixed period. The majority of the farmers, whose milk had already been coming to Maryland Farm for cheesemaking through the auspices of the MMB or Milk Marque, were pleased to sign contracts.

Barbers had a reputation as a successful cheese making business and they too were farmers and understood the uncertainty that farmers were feeling at the time. Purchasing milk was a very complicated business, they were competing with other cheesemakers on price and yet their customers were reluctant to accept an increase in the price of cheese. As cheese sales increased Barbers acquired more milk producers on fixed contracts.

More Expansion

In 1971 Hugh Leir died in Canada and his eldest son Richard inherited the estate in Ditcheat. He came to England and announced that he would now sell what was left of the estate, the Priory, Abbey Farm, the outbuildings and the last sixty acres. Abbey Farm was not only part of the business but it was the house where generations of Barbers had been born and brought up. Cheesemaking had taken place in a large copper vat in a room which is now the dining room. In 1945 cheesemaking ceased at Abbey Farm.

The company bought the estate for £80,000. Now the Barbers owned Abbey Farm and the last sixty acres. The Priory was in need of considerable restoration but had a long history and was in an idyllic position on the edge of the village. It was sold to Sir Christopher Chancellor for £29,000.

Management meetings took place, and still do, on the third Wednesday in the month. It was recognised that income and expenditure should be analysed on a more professional basis than previously. Decimalisation of the British currency was blamed for inflation.

The accounts analysis of the previous month for each section of the business were carefully scrutinised, problems were discussed and decisions taken. Four cheque books were used, one for each section of the business; Farms, Pigs, Dairy, and Sales. Like most family businesses there were times when the family disagreed and in the late 1960's Michael Cozens of Palmer Snell Estate Agents (later Michael Bonham Cozens), was invited to become an Executive Chairman and would chair the monthly meetings. Michael brought a wealth of experience to the Boardroom meetings which then ran smoothly. When Michael stepped down Major Dick Hargreaves M.C. (4th Parachute Battalion), past Chairman of Devonish Breweries, who had a good understanding of commerce, accepted the position but when Dick retired the Board considered there was no longer any requirement for an Executive Chairman.

Valerie Boothman joined A J & RG Barber as a Farm Secretary in 1972. On her first day Paul Barber came into the office and asked had she seen the insemination gun. It was a piece of equipment she was not familiar with but it brought home to her very quickly that she was working for farmers.

In the afternoon she answered the telephone to a London customer who asked for 12 cases of Caerphilly wheels. She asked the Office Manager how she would know that there *was* a stock of Caerphilly wheels. He explained that she should go down the office stairs, up two steps, turn sharp left, then left again and then slide open the heavy cold store door on the right and count them.

When she suggested that she should introduce a stock system and she would record the cheese made each day and deduct the cheese sold and keep running totals there was no objection. She also persuaded the directors to purchase a mechanical calculator so that the well thumbed little "Ready Reckoner" could be retired. Invoices were hand written with carbon copies retained. Accounts were not computerised until 1988. Very soon Val started to assist Farmer Gerald with cheese sales.

Since the late 1960's, Peter Green Haulage of Evercreech had taken over deliveries of Barbers cheese to all parts of the country. In 1972 Barbers decided to offer cold storage, cutting and packing and a distribution facility to importer Barry Thorne of Rowson & Co., of Tooley Street, London. Peter Green Haulage co-operated by undertaking the additional distribution responsibilities. Each week approximately twenty tons of 4x5 kgs of cheddar packed in Rowson "Rosewood" labels were despatched to their depot in London and a further thirty tons would be sent out as individual one ton orders to all parts of the country.

One day in 1982 Barbers received a special request from Barry Thorne to cut and pack twenty tons for the Falkland Islands. When the girls in the packing plant learnt that the destination of the cheese they were packing was to the troops in the Falklands they immediately rushed out to the village shop, bought greeting cards, wrote good luck messages on them and packed them in the cases with the cheese. One assumes the gesture was much appreciated when the cheese arrived in the South Atlantic.

On one occasion Barry Thorne asked if Barbers could take a delivery of sixty tons of French Cheddar direct from France on a Goods Train. This would save considerable costs of handling and road haulage. Val contacted British Rail in Westbury, Wiltshire, who were responsible for Goods Trains in the South West.

At that time there was a railway siding at Castle Cary Station and after much discussion it was agreed that if the train came in during the evening and "parked up" in the siding, the cheese would have to be unloaded by 12 noon the next day as the train must then depart. During the evening Nicky and Val went down to the Station to watch the Goods Train arrive. The next morning, at the crack of dawn, anything on wheels was sent down to the Station and staff were drawn from all sections of the Company to man handle 20 kg blocks of "Centre Cheddar" on to small lorries, trailers pulled by tractors, carts, in fact no vehicle was too small. In the end Peter Green Haulage also helped with the task. By midday all 3000 x 20 kg blocks of French Cheddar were safely stored in Ditcheat Cold Stores and the Goods train departed.

On another occasion Barbers stored several tons of Belgian Cheddar made by a co-operative of farmers in Belgium. Their importer arranged a coach trip to Somerset for all the farmers and their wives as they wished to see where their cheese was stored and also asked that lunch be laid on for them in the Manor House Inn in the village. They helped themselves to a very substantial buffet and when different puddings were offered and they were asked which one they would like to eat, the answer was "yes, yes, yes, yes" to all of them. They had good appetites but left well satisfied.

In 1974 Robert Vincent decided to sell *Lower Wraxall*. The farm had been in his family for generations but it was in need of investment and Robert decided to sell up and purchase another farm in south Somerset. *Lower Wraxall* adjoined the *Ringwell Milking Unit*, land already owned by Barbers so the farm was purchased. Field drainage schemes were created, more cows were stocked and the farmhouse was available for the herdsman and his family.

Growth of Cheese Sales and Further Expansion

Sadly Farmer Gerald died in 1978 at the age of 62. For six years Val Boothman had been working with him on cheese sales and he had been able to allow her to take over many of his responsibilities. Val was promoted to Sales Manager and later she was invited to join the Board. There was an excellent demand for Barbers Maryland Farmhouse Mature Cheddar and through the strict grading system only the best cheddar was sold under that brand name.

It was decided that any cheese not suitable for the Farmhouse label would be sold under a different brand name. This protected the high reputation of Maryland Farmhouse Cheddar. As sales of cheese were growing faster than production the company decided to buy cheese from other producers, pack it and sell it under another brand label and thereby accommodate customers who wished to purchase different qualities at different prices for *their* customers.

Previously customers had bought the best Farmhouse Cheddar from Barbers and went elsewhere for cheaper and milder products. The brand names Haystack Tasty and Haystack Mild became very popular and were a welcome addition to the Maryland Farm label on the price lists. Cheese produced elsewhere had to be very carefully graded and selected and the skills of Trevor Vaughan who had been trained to be a Cheese

Grader (and was also Store Manager) were important. Cheese Graders are traditionally promoted and trained from within the company. Their skills are vital.

Many Ditcheat families have generations who have worked for the company. A typical example is Shaun Smith who after school each day and on Saturday mornings would earn spending money helping to tidy the loading bay, carry cheeses and despatch orders. When he left Sexeys Grammar School age 17 in 1979 he joined the company full time working in many capacities in the Cold Store, involved in Cold Store Management, export orders and cheese grading. He is still working at Barbers in 2012. His mother, brothers and sister were also employees.

As the business flourished and relationships with Supermarkets strengthened, Barbers had the courage to increase their acreage and Knowle *Park* farm adjoining Wincanton Race Course was purchased in 1979. Paul Barber's enthusiasm for farming was essential as more farms were acquired. The next generation of Barbers committed themselves to the business and the dairy capacity increased to make more cheese. *Highbridge Farm* was acquired in 1984; *Lower Farm* (Sutton), in 2003 and *Longwoods* (Wraxall) was purchased from the Look family in 2004.

Pigs

Dairy farmers who made cheese had surplus whey to dispose of and for generations this whey was fed to pigs so many dairy farmers were also pig farmers. Maryland Farm was no different. Pigs were fattened at Maryland Farm until 1990 when the buildings were demolished to make way for more milk silos and a new pig unit was erected at Moor Lane a few miles outside the village.

Visits from the Supermarket Buyers proved difficult when they had questioned the site of the pigs at Maryland Farm and the proximity to the dairy where cheese was being made. For years they were assured that the whiff from the pigs was what gave the cheddar that very special flavour but inevitably the Buyers became more difficult to convince and the pigs had to be found another home. Farmer Jack was a passionate Pig Farmer and had a reputation for being a good one. He always had great respect for the pig and used to say that the only part of a pig you could not eat was its squeak. He was exasperated by the imports of bacon and hams from abroad which damaged the home market.

In 1981 Penn Barn Farm in Dorset (587 acres) was purchased A further responsibility for Paul. A modern pig fattening unit was built which still operates in 2012. The farm also produces arable crops and sheep are grazed.

Bagborough Farm pig breeding unit sited between Ditcheat and Shepton Mallet closed in 1997. It was no longer a viable part of the business. In 1990 the company purchased land just outside Wiveliscombe in the south of the County, initially planning to build a second cheese making dairy. At the time Barbers were struggling to purchase sufficient milk for the Ditcheat operation through the Milk Marketing Board and it was suggested by the MMB that a base near to Taunton could be allocated a substantial milk quota for cheese making.

When it became apparent that this could not be guaranteed the company decided to build a "state of the art" new pig abattoir where the Wiltshire curing method would take place. Bacon and hams would be produced and sold direct to the major buyers. The success of making and maturing a high quality cheese had proved successful in the cheese trade but this venture into the pig slaughtering and curing market was quite different.

This contemporary pig processing factory was stifled by regulations which did not apply to older abattoirs with which the company competed. Consequently overheads were much higher than competitors and although the product was accepted in the trade as being of exceptional quality, few were prepared to pay the price required to make the operation profitable. The abattoir was sold in 1995.

The History of the Industry, its Decline and Survival

This family farming and cheesemaking business is part of a thriving Somerset farming and Farmhouse Cheesemaking industry. It would be wrong not to provide a wider picture. This chapter explains the history of the industry and how it has survived although many Farmhouse Cheesemakers have been less fortunate.

The word "tradition" would be defined in the dictionary of a Farmhouse Cheesemaker as a custom and skill handed down from father to son through generations. Not only the skill of the Cheesemaker but the successful continuing cycle of the dairy farm.

To keep a sense of proportion and perspective we will look at traditional cheesemaking and associated farm activities during three separate years, each two decades apart. The figures quoted are based on the best information currently available though in some of the earlier instances records are sparse to say the least and adjustments have been made to iron out abnormal seasonal fluctuations.

1935

There were 1150 farmers making traditional cheese in Britain. They produced 30% of all cheese manufactured in the UK. Imported cheese accounted for 85% of cheese consumed in Britain. The average cheese making farm was usually approximately 100 acres but rarely exceeded 200 acres. Short horn cows were the prominent breed but a few Ayrshire and Friesian cows were slowly being introduced in an attempt to raise milk yields. Horses played an important role but tractors and stationary engines were beginning to change farming practices.

Milking machines were being introduced and the bail in the fields and the bucket plant in the cow sheds led to much improved productivity. General milk hygiene moved forward and keeping quality increased with cooling taking place to the temperature of the main's water supply. 17 gallon churns gave way to 12 or 10 gallon churns. The cheesemaking, which was a late Spring to early Autumn operation, took place in a dairy located in a ground floor room of the large farmhouse. Cheese was stored either above the dairy, or during a hot summer, in the cellar. The farmer's wife or a female member of the family usually made the cheese though in some instances a Cheesemaker was employed.

Cheesemaking equipment consisted of a round copper vat up to 250 gallon capacity fitted with a steam jacket, a coal or wood fired steam raiser (known in Somerset as apparatus), a cooler peg mill, vertical presses, moulds, knives, buckets, sterilising chests, washing troughs, etc. There was no electricity to lighten the work in the early days and cheese weighing up to 1 cwt (50 kgs) each were normal. Much devoted work went into the making of each cheese which were generally of good quality although some farms were particularly renowned for their regular high quality make. Cheesemakers dreaded the monthly visit of the Cheese Grader to the farm and there were many devious practices to disguise the activity of a mouse or a tainted cheese.

The grading process was strict. Matured Farmhouse Cheddar (no less than 9 month maturity) was sold at a price 10% above comparable British Cheese. Whey was considered a valuable asset and together with a suitable ration from the nearest pig feed mill, was fed to the pigs which were fattened for bacon. Pig manures spread on the land were much used as fertiliser for growing more grass for cows.

1955

There were only 125 farmers making cheese in Britain in 1955. They produced 6% of all cheese manufactured in the UK. Imported cheese accounted for 70% consumed in Britain. The Second World War and agricultural economics generally had drastically reduced the number of cheese making farmers and only the larger producers remained.

The dogged determination of the surviving cheesemakers to stay in business, despite decreasing viability, demanded a new approach to cheesemaking on farms. The first steps were taken to increase manufacture by investing in new dairies and purchasing extra milk from adjoining farms. New dairies were built, often by converting disused stables, to cope with the greater amount of milk available to increase cheese production. The advancement of dairy technology created exciting labour saving equipment such as 1000 gallon vats and mechanical agitators. Cheesemakers were now employed men who had learnt their craft from the farmer and helpers of both sexes adapted readily to new ideas. With increased production the decline in output bottomed out.

Milk, being produced largely from Friesian cows much improved from the use of Artificial Insemination (AI) from proven bulls, was less prone to seasonal fluctuations and cheese was made the year round. Good advice from the National Agricultural Advisory Service, the use of mineral fertilisers, improved strains of grasses, machines designed around the tractor and increased stocking rates, brought increased milk production from each farm. Milk samples were taken by Farmhouse Cheesemakers for the first time and tested for compositional and hygiene quality, the latter with either resazurin or methylene blue.

The process of cheesemaking now demanded changes of emphasis in order to accommodate milk from different farms and makers increased quantities of starter culture to 1% and ripened for one hour to maintain control over the cheese manufacturing time. Now whey, before going to pigs, was separated and butter made from the cream was usually sold at the farm or local produce market.

The cheeses being produced in 1955 were cylindrical and regular in shape weighing 56 lbs (26 kgs) and were stored on wooden shelves in the traditional way. Grading cheese was followed by maturing in store and the final marketing was usually undertaken by The Milk Marketing Board. Farmhouse Mature Cheddar Cheese was sold at a price 16% above comparable British Cheese at this time. This much increased price differential may to some extent be explained by reduced quantities of Farmhouse Cheese available.

1975

The number of Farmhouse Cheesemakers in Britain had now reduced to 52. They produced 10% of cheese manufactured in the UK. Imported cheese accounted for 40% of cheese consumed in Britain. The smaller number of Farmhouse Cheesemakers should not be confused with a decline in the industry, quite the contrary.

The quantity of cheese being made annually on farms with the farmers own milk production and that of "bought in" milk from other West Country farms was greater than ever before. A quiet revolution in agricultural practices was responsible for increased output, and the farm with a stock of 100 cows each averaging 1000 gallons of milk per lactation was commonplace.

Two herdsmen, with modern equipment, were now able to milk, feed, and clean out milking units for 200 cows daily. Cubicle housing, ad. lib. grass or silage, balanced concentrates and lowering of disease levels led to cows producing an increased quantity of cleaner and higher quality milk. Herring-bone or rotary parlours, coupled to refrigerated bulk tanks, with a boiling acid or chemical sterilising system, provided cowmen with much improved milking equipment.

Farmhouse cheesemaking dairies kept pace with modern machinery and bulk handling and storage of milk allowed employees in cheesemaking to reduce to a 5½ day week. Pasteurizers would often deliver milk into 2,500 gallon vats. Oil and gas fired boilers of varying designs became the standard means of raising steam and uses for high pressure compressed air were and are many and varied.

In 1975 Farmhouse Mature Cheddar was sold at a premium of 14%. Traditional Cylindrical Farmhouse Cheddar Cheese accounted for about 50% of Farmhouse Cheddar production but times were changing. The housewife was now buying her food mainly from Supermarkets and they required the same high quality cheese but in pre-packed form. Consequently 50% was now produced as 20 kgs rindless blocks which could easily be cut and packed into uniform 250 gm and 500gm pieces.

 The Somerset Farmhouse Cheesemaker continues to move with the times albeit protecting the traditions of the industry. In 2012 there are fewer Farmhouse Cheesemakers but those who have survived have hugely increased production.

Most farms have their own laboratories ensuring that tests on milk and cheese are carried out daily and immediately when necessary. Plate counts, psychotropic counts, tests for butter fats and solids-not-fats tests give the Cheesemaker greater knowledge of his raw material.

The increased production of cheese presented the requirement for sophisticated effluent treatment plants and the inherent capital costs. Whey is now a valuable commodity and the investment in whey processing plants provide the farmer with the possibility of maximising production efficiency

Introducing Automation in the Dairy

Due to a great demand for Barbers 20kg rindless blocks of Farmhouse Mature Cheddar the dairy was extended and capacity increased. Traditionally Cheddar was made in open vats where the junket was cut into curds and whey and scalded for two hours. Thereafter the curds and whey gravitated to the cooler for the final drainage.

This is where the hard work began with the cutting, turning, and stacking of the "loaves" of curd. One ton of curd would be turned by hand five or six times before being fed into a mill and hand salted.

The whole process took four and a half hours before moulding up. The curd was pressed into prepared rectangular metal moulds lined with cheese cloths and closed with lids. The moulds were then placed on presses overnight to drain surplus whey.

The next day the cheese were tipped out of the moulds and wrapped in film and waxed paper, sealed in a Flowers Press, boxed in wooden boxes and palletised to be taken to the Cold Store for maturing. The cheesemaking process was labour intensive and as production increased there was much absenteeism through back complaints. It became very difficult to employ young men prepared to work for long hours doing such work. This system was both laborious and time consuming.

For some time Nicky had been toying with an idea to introduce some automation into the system to alleviate the physical side of the operation while still requiring the skill of the Cheesemaker. In 1989 Nicky contacted Wincanton Engineering, a local cheesemaking equipment manufacturer and arranged a meeting to discuss his ideas only to be told that proper engineering drawings costing £35,000 would have to be produced before they could quote for the work.

Nicky was confident, boosted by necessity, that it would work without affecting the quality of the cheese. The system consisted of a draining belt with wires to cut the "loaves" of curds from the moving mat and automatically make the first turn onto a transfer belt, leading to the "cheddaring" belt where the curd was further turned and stacked but this time by hand.

The final turn "by hand" in the process is the requirement of the "Protection of Origin" status. (Legislation came into force in 1994 to protect the reputation of certain regional foods such as Parma Ham, Champagne and Melton Mowbray Pork Pies).

The turning belt fed the curd mill and curd was transferred to the salting belt and then fed to the mould filler and presses. The new "belt" system was installed in 1989 and proved to be remarkably successful. Barbers continued to use the individual moulds but were still looking at new systems.

As demand and thereby production increased many Farmhouse Cheesemakers upgraded their system from individual moulds to the continuous block former system. In this system curd is drawn into towers under vacuum which creates pressure by the weight of a vertical column of curd. Whey is siphoned off as it collects in the tower at the base of which is a guillotine system called a "block" former.

A "block" is cut from the stack at regular intervals and pushed away to be packaged in a nylon poly bag and stored in wooden boxes under temperature control for a minimum of nine months. The same careful grading system takes place during maturation to protect the brand West Country Farmhouse Mature Cheddar.

Peter Horner joined the company as Dairy Manager in 1989 and was enthusiastic for Barbers to introduce block formers which would replace the individual moulds and much machinery. Block formers were introduced in 1990 to 1991. The original "towers" were purchased from Alpha Laval, cheesemaking equipment manufactures and they were made in New Zealand. They started being replaced in 2002 with the Wincanton tall towers. The taller the tower, the greater capacity to cope with increased production. Wincanton vats were replaced in 2004 with Tetra OST vats.

The Pre-Packing Plant

The cheese market was changing and it was essential to be selling considerable tonnages to major supermarkets. For many years Barbers had sold cheese to Sainsburys to be cut and packed in their packing plant under Sainsburys own label. In 1989 when Sainsburys decided to close down their packing plant and purchase cheese in pre-packed form it was a blow to Barbers. The company desperately needed to continue supplying their Farmhouse Mature Cheddar and fortunately Sainsburys also wished the supply to continue.

Barbers cheese was sold as "Sainsburys West Country Farmhouse Mature Cheddar", own label and they considered it to be a "destination product". This description was explained to the company by Sainsbury's Buyer. It meant that they considered some housewives visited Sainsburys stores purposely to buy this product and whilst there, would purchase other food.

Nicky went to Sainsburys Head Office at Stamford House for a meeting with their Buyer. Whilst he was there a fire alarm sounded and everyone had to vacate their offices and congregate at a special point outside the building.

Nicky chatted to a man whom he discovered was a director and whilst waiting to re-enter the building Nicky explained who he was and mentioned the problem that had arisen. The director then suggested that this could be solved to everyone's benefit if Barbers purchased the cutting and packing plant from J Sainsbury in

Basingstoke. A deal was struck within the next few weeks. Not only the equipment but their Packing Plant manger Bill Leach would transfer to Ditcheat. The main cold store had to be extended, the loss of another orchard and a state of the art packing room created. This was a huge investment and thanks to Bill Leach and the dedication of existing and new staff it became a great success.

At this time Barbers were selling cheese to Sainsburys and Tesco but had lost a contract with Waitrose who had been good customer's years before. The Ilchester Cheese Company, as it was then, also purchased large amounts each week. They were the second largest customer behind Sainsburys. When Ilchester exhibited at the food fair at Annuga in Cologne, Val and Nicky supported their Managing Director John Davidge, by flying out to Germany to help "man the stand".

The interpreters John had employed were not only expert translators but were good saleswomen and as Val and Nicky did not speak a word of German, other than "nein, nein" and "der kase" they were not required so spent a pleasant afternoon in Cologne cathedral. Fortunately the cathedral had not been bombed during the war as the British pilots used the twin towers as a land mark to get their bearings.

The trip to Cologne did not seem to have been a waste of time as it was interesting to visit the thirteen food and drink halls at Annuga and enjoy John's hospitality in the evening. Ilchester also exhibited at food fairs in Barcelona "Alimentaria" and shared a stand with Barbers on one occasion.

They also exhibited at "Sial" in Paris on a regular basis.

Bill Hornby, who joined the company in July 1986, looked after the Tesco account and at one time they purchased Red Leicester Cheese and Double Gloucester Cheese on a weekly basis. That contract was eventually lost to Helers in Cheshire but Tesco continued to purchase Maryland Farmhouse Mature Vintage Cheddar.

The Agricultural and Cheese Shows had for a long time been a vehicle for cheesemakers to exhibit their products and enter competitions and the winners gained much publicity. The Frome Cheese Show, The Royal Bath and West Show, The Nantwich International Cheese Show and The Shepton Mallet Agricultural Show were events in the calendar important to all West Country Farmhouse Cheesemakers.

On the day Bill started his employment, Barbers had decided to exhibit at the Nantwich Show as well as competing in the different classes and Bill offered to help Val. The day before the Show started exhibitors had to transfer their cheeses from the boots of cars to the marquee and erect their stand. Nantwich, unlike The Bath and West Show, is held in an agricultural field and had no tarmac paths and it poured with rain.

Bill borrowed a sack trolley and battled through the horrendous mud. By the time the stand was erected and all the cheeses stacked in an attractive display, Bill and Val looked like waifs and strays. It had taken hours to reach the end of their task and it had stopped raining. Bill disappeared for ten minutes and then reappeared with two cups of steaming hot coffee and two bacon rolls. It was like nectar from the Gods.

The company had a wide customer base with many small customers buying one or two tons a week. This was good profitable business although it was inevitable that this business would decrease as more cheese was purchased by the housewife through the supermarkets.

One day Val Boothman received a 'phone call from a cheese Creamery in Ireland to ask if she was interested in purchasing 50 tons of mature Irish Cheddar at a good price. It sounded very interesting so Val flew from Bristol to Dublin the next day. She was met at the airport by a chauffeur who deposited her at a hotel in Wexford and she was told she would be collected at 9 am the next day.

On arrival at the Creamery she was given a cup of coffee whilst she waited and waited. Eventually the Creamery Manager arrived and was very embarrassed when he admitted that they had "lost" the 50 tons of Cheddar. They could not find it anywhere. It was suggested that rather than the visit be a total waste of time she may like to look at some other cheese. Later that day she purchased 40 tons of young but very "tasty" cheddar at an extremely good price which was eventually sold by the company under a new name, Haystack Tasty.

Farmer Jack had gradually passed full management of the farms and pigs to Paul. Paul's eldest son Chris (born 1966) had been committed to the business since early school days and there was never any doubt that on leaving school he would be the first of the next generation of Barbers to join the company. In 1984 he went to America for a couple of years to gain experience of farming and managerial skills and to broaden his horizons. He worked on rice and almond farms north of Sacramento near to Arbuckle. Paul's younger son Giles (born 1968) had left University having gained his degree in Sales and Marketing and was gaining experience in other fields.

Chris remembers his grandfather (Farmer Jack) telling him a story about *his* father Alfred. When he was a young man he used to herd the stock to market in Shepton Mallet whilst sitting on a horse drawn cart. This journey was about six miles through the lanes from Ditcheat. There he would meet other farming friends and when all their stock had been sold they would retire to the bar parlour in The Market Inn to quench their thirsts; the very same bar parlour where his grandfather had met his friends many years previously.

How long it took to quench their thirsts was not part of the story but when Alfred came out of the Inn he would climb aboard his horse and cart and instruct the horse to take him home to Ditcheat. When the farmers were no longer allowed to drive their stock to market through the lanes, one of the farm workers took them in a farm truck and Alfred followed by car. The very first time he drove to market in his car he enjoyed a drink as usual with his friends. On the way home the car ran into a hedge. He had never had this problem with the horse.

Nicky's two sons Charles (born 1972) and Anthony (born 1974) also worked outside the business at first but after University Charlie joined the Sales team at the Pig Meat processing plant in Wiveliscombe and when that was sold joined the Sales and Management team at Ditcheat. Val Boothman had been appointed to the board of Directors in 1993 but in 2003 was preparing to retire and Giles Barber agreed to join the company and work with her and Charlie. The three worked together closely until Val retired.

Anthony followed Nicky's direction learning how to make cheese and dairy management and worked closely with Peter Horner. As Anthony's responsibilities increased Peter was appointed Operations Manager allowing him to concentrate on product management and the whey plant. By the time Peter retired in 2008 Anthony was Dairy Manager but Peter continued to be available as a consultant when and if required. Chris Barber inevitably took over full management of the farms.

Chris Newcombe joined Barbers in January 2002 as Chief Accountant bringing his professionalism into the finances of the company and was later appointed to the Board as Financial Director. When Val retired in 2003, Paul and Nicky were also starting to reduce their responsibilities and the next generation were proving very capable of taking the reins. The relationship with J Sainsbury Limited continued to gain strength as did that with Norseland, previously Ilchester Cheese Company and other major supermarkets were beginning to show interest.

The West of England and South Wales Provision Trade Association

For many years before 1887 Britain's buyers and sellers of (mostly imported) bacon, ham, lard, butter, cheese and canned meat had constituted what they considered an exclusive section of the food trade – the provision trade. In London it was conducted on the quays and markets between London Bridge and the Tower of London, first on the north bank of the Thames and before the turn of the century on the south – in Tooley Street.

When Britain's population outgrew its ability to feed itself London based agents took over from Irish and West Country farmers as the main source of London's food supply and London's importers and wholesalers, who were their customers, established the Home and Foreign Produce Exchange as a provision market and trade association to agree minimum prices, regulate the trade and limit competition.

During the "Golden Age" of English farming from 1853 to 1870 little attention had been given to dairying in spite of the development of cattle and the formation of pedigree herds. In the West Country there was rapid conversion of the land from mixed farming to dairying over the thirty years 1871 to 1901. The number of agricultural labourers fell from 962,000 to 621,000. Six million acres were added to permanent pasture land between 1866 and 1911. It was too little too late as in spite of these efforts home production was nowhere near enough to meet the demand of a ballooning population. The Food Exchanges in the capital and the regions were established.

In July 1910 "Manchester" suggested that all such regional bodies should be federated and a year later "Bristol" invited all parties to a meeting to discuss the matter but no such meeting took place. In the early 1970's The London Exchange members discussed becoming a federation or association and on March 1ˢᵗ 1976 "The United Kingdom Provision Trade Federation" came into being. Eventually the regional exchanges became affiliated and the Bristol Exchange was now called The West of England and South Wales Provision Trade Association.

In 1985 Arthur Hamilton of Lye Cross Farm invited Barbers to join the Association. It had been in existence since 1883 as the Bristol Exchange. Originally membership had been restricted to the West Country but gradually the Committee agreed to include South Wales.

Cheese and dairy products dominate the proceedings at the meetings but dairy companies and ancillary businesses from many parts of the UK applied for membership and were made welcome. The membership grew to include companies from northern counties, the midlands and the Home Counties as well as the West Country and South Wales.

Barbers membership put them in touch with a much broader

market place and their name became known throughout the cheese trade. Val Boothman represented Barbers at these meetings and after serving as Secretary to the Association was elected Chairman in 1992. She was the first woman to hold the position. The company continue to support the Association; Linda Adams of Barbers has served as Secretary for many years and in 2010 Giles Barber was elected Chairman.

Giles continues to represent the Company at the meetings. Most of the regional Provision Exchanges or Associations have their own Golf Societies. A group of members of the London Exchange established their Golf Society in 1910 and justified it by saying that it was "to relieve the pressures of the working day and banish thoughts of pending insolvency". It is still thriving in 2012.

The Golf Society attached to the West of England and South Wales Provision Trade Association also has a long history. For some years it lay dormant but in 1992 a few interested members held a meeting at The Mendip Golf Club and revived it. In 2012 it is the most successful and best supported of all the Golf Societies in the Provision Trade. Charlie Barber has served on the Executive Committee for several years and although Val Boothman has retired she still organises the Golfing Society Annual events and holds the position of Treasurer and Secretary.

Channel Islands

In 1991 Richard Allan set up an agency in the Channel Islands with Bob Parker, a Jerseyman, under the name Parkallan Ltd. They had both worked for Kraft Foods on the mainland at one time. Bob had actually retired but Richard needed his involvement in order to create a Jersey based company. He approached Peter and Paul Williams in London who operated under the name Rustic Cheese Company and they suggested he contacted Barbers.

Richard had good contacts in the Channel Islands and was already selling other products but needed a supplier of good quality cheese. Barbers agreed to supply him and he would receive a commission on sales. The main customer was Le Riche who had several stores and Cash and Carry depots in Jersey and Guernsey. They were the "Marks and Spencer" of the Channel Islands. Maryland Farm Cheddar became the main brand of cheese sold on the islands although there was stiff opposition from other large manufacturers.

The customers were pleased to see Richard every week and he would check their shelves and write out his own orders, it was very relaxed. However about twice a year they expected personal attention from Barbers. It was all very old fashioned and they naturally liked attention from Ditcheat whatever their size of business.

On these occasions Val flew over from Bristol and many times

Diana Barber accompanied her. Usually the smaller customers didn't quite understand that Diana was Nicky's wife, they thought she was in "Sales". You could be in a meeting with a director of Le Riche, discussing the cost of television advertising for Maryland Farm Cheddar on Channel Island Television at 11 am and at 1 pm you could be sitting in a garage converted into an office, on a chair, drinking "builder's tea. Everyone was very friendly.

On another occasion, a cold February morning, they had to wait whilst the airport staff scraped ice from the Aurigny Air Services small sixteen-seater plane which was to transfer them to Guernsey to visit customers there. Some passengers boarded the plane from the left side and some from the right. The eight double seats seemed so small and cosy that they were astounded when the passenger in the front seat turned out to be the pilot. The name of the small yellow plane was Trislander, pronounced "trylander" which did not fill nervous passengers with too much confidence. Their fears were unfounded.

Barbers supplied and visited a wide spectrum of cheese customers in the Channel Islands, some were quite small businesses but others purchased a considerable tonnage. Le Riche were eventually taken over by another company involved with Waitrose which reduced the quantity Barbers would sell to Le Riche but in 2012 they still supply small Le Riche stores, Easenmyne, the Co-op, Alliance, Battrick and others. The customers have always been very loyal to the brand name Maryland Farm.

Exports - Spain

In 1998 Barbers started exporting cheese to Spain. Originally to small supermarkets through a Distributor called Esteve Quera of Figueras.

It became obvious that if exports were to expand they needed professional help. Barbers contacted the Food from Britain office in London and were then introduced to Guillermo Alvares de Lorenzano the Director of Food from Britain in Madrid. He arranged meetings in several towns in Spain and he and Val visited companies in Malaga, Valencia, Barcelona and Madrid. From these meetings business started with COTOLOSA in Malaga and DOMPAL in Madrid.

Other companies were considered but at the time Señor Juan Carlos Tejero the MD of Dompal, who were huge Serrano and Iberico Ham manufacturers and curers, was keen to start importing English cheese and had a strong sales force covering Madrid and Barcelona. In fact Juan Carlos would claim that his company covered all of Spain!

Cotolosa too seemed sound people to deal with. The Company was owned by the Torres family who were very interested in horses and visited Ditcheat to see Maryland Farm but were more interested in Paul Nicholls Racing Stables. Their stores in Malaga were stocked with many UK products such as Chevas Regal Whiskey, Gordons Gin, and Carrs Water Biscuits. Unfortunately Barbers suffered a financial set back with them as they failed to pay their account, having suffered a bad debt themselves.

The company exhibited regularly at Alimentaria in Barcelona, the third largest European Food Fair after Sial and Annuga. The export team included Val Boothman, Linda Adams, Charlie Barber and Ramon Fito. Ramon had responsibilities in the dairy at Maryland but as he was Spanish it was decided he would be very useful as part of the team. Ramon was far more than an interpreter as his personality and character came to the fore and he was very popular with all visitors to the stand. The first time he helped to man the stand the visitors queried his position.

The next day it was decided he should use a Business Card printing machine he had seen in the subway and he became "Maryland Farm Production Manager". It was instant promotion. Many possible customers were very impressed to think that this English Farmhouse Cheese company had a Spanish person in such a high position. One year at Alimentaria, the stand was visited by Vincente and Victor Parra, father and son, whose business was called Exclusiva Procomercio based in Alicante. They were very enthusiastic about importing English food, in fact anything English. They became very regular customers.

When Val decided to retire it was agreed that Giles Barber would take over exports. Val, Giles and Ramon flew to Madrid to introduce Giles to Juan Carlos, MD of DOMPAL. During their visit they all attended a reception for the British Ambassador to Madrid before leaving for Alicante.

The next day they were due to fly from Alicante to Bristol at 1 pm. The account of what happened that morning will never be recounted without Giles and Ramon shaking with laughter. As they had time to kill, Val suggested that she visited the hairdresser and the boys could spend time in Alicante before they were all due to leave for the airport. Ramon directed her to one not far away. Val was carrying a small English/Spanish dictionary and she checked what the words were for "blow dry". It clearly said "moldeado" so this is what she asked for. She had to wait some time before the hairdresser started and then became alarmed as the lady started putting her hair in small metal curlers and damping the hair with what smelt like perm lotion. In despair Val kept saying "smooth, smooth, no permanente" to no avail.

The hairdresser kept saying "Si si si". In a state of panic she phoned Ramon on her mobile phone and said he must get over to her as quickly as possible as there was a massive problem. When they arrived Ramon tried to help and there was considerable confusion. Apparently "moldeado" means "perm" not "blow dry". She should have said " lavado y secado", quite different.

The boys said they would wait in the street and when Val emerged her hair style was now a wet blonde afro. In fact Giles described the style as looking like a wet poodle. It looked as though she had suffered an electric shock. The boys pretended they were looking into the shop window opposite with their backs to Val but they were shaking with laughter which they were trying to control. They gave her a big hug with tears streaming down their cheeks.

They looked for a hat shop and Val purchased a denim trilby which she rammed on her head. There followed much leg pulling which Val tried to find amusing. Comments such as "you can't go on the plane wearing that hat, they will think you are hiding a gun" and other such helpful comments. On returning to England Val had to visit the hairdressers three or four times a week to have her hair straightened until it grew out. She wrote to the publishers complaining about the error in the dictionary but received no reply.

The company continue to export cheese to Spain and have a strong relationship with Juan Carlos Tejero (DOMPAL) who has visited Ditcheat many times with his family.

HRH The Countess of Wessex opening the new laboratories and coldstore extension at Maryland Farm. 21st March 2012

Anthony Barber escorting HRH The Countess of Wessex March 2012

HRH The Countess of Wessex learning about the curd from David Miller

HRH The Countess of Wessex enjoying a joke with Shaun Smith

Val Boothman joins the Board of Directors 1993

Food Fair in Barcelona 1996

Giles, Señor Juan Carlos Tejero, Val, Sonia and Ramon Fito.

The Sales Team 1999
Adrian Bennett, Bill Horny, Val Boothman, Jon Cox, Charlie Barber

Maryland Farm and coldstores nestle into the Somerset countryside.

Maryland Farm Offices 2012

Maryland Farm c.1965 with the "New" dairy in the foreground.

Maryland Farm 2012

Maryland Farm c. 1980

The tractor shed with ancient and modern.

The farm shop at Maryland Farm.

The original Maryland Farmhouse inset and how it is utilised as the workshop in 2012

Denman and Paul, the best of friends.

Denman winning The Cheltenham Gold Cup 2007

"The girls coming home for milking". Meadow milking unit 2012.

The milk receiving area, Maryland Farm, Ditcheat. August 2012.

Nicky Barber - "The Master Grader"

The "1833" Cheese Course

Barbers 1833 Vintage Reserve Cheddar - A success story

Maryland Farmhouse Butter

Abbey Farm, Ditcheat. August 2012.

The Tythe barn, Abbey Farm, Ditcheat. August 2012.

Manor Farm, Ditcheat. August 2012.

Manor Farm racing stables during the close season. August 2012.

Prospect House, Ditcheat. August 2012.

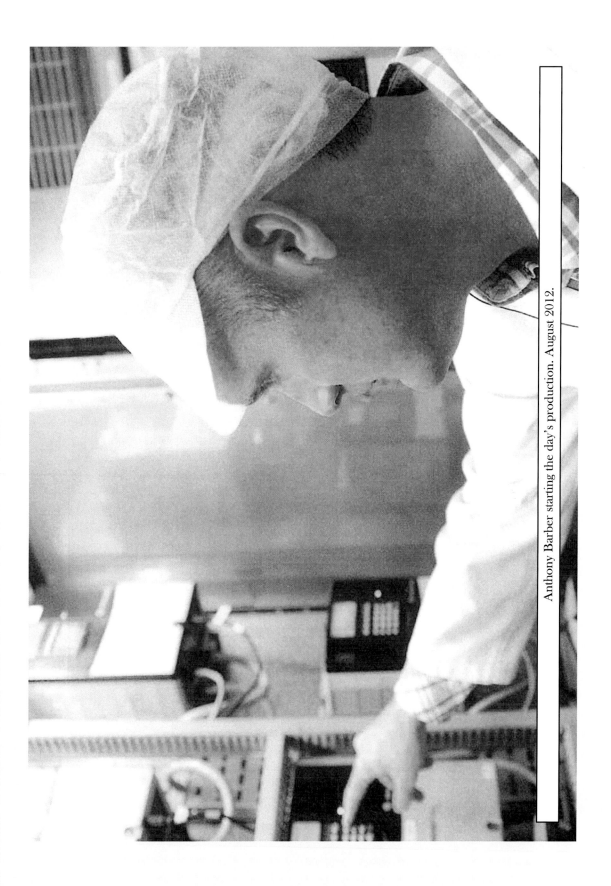

Anthony Barber starting the day's production. August 2012.

The Next Generation. Back row: Catherine, Ollie, Alfie, Ellen, Maddie. Front row: Lola, Flora, Tilly, Mai, Hannah. August 2012

Nicky, Val and Paul. 1999.

Fathers & Sons. Chris, Giles, Paul, Nicky, Charlie and Anthony. August 2012.

Somerdale International Limited

In 2009 the company started exporting cheese to America through Somerdale, leading UK exporters of British cheese and dairy products, based in Wellington, Somerset. There had been a long relationship with the Managing Director Stephen Jones going back to his early days when he was the Export Director for Dairyvale (Exports) Ltd. In 2011 approximately 300 tonnes of Barber and Somerdale own label was exported to the States and in 2012 the market to Australia, China and the Far East is expanding. Somerdale are one of the largest exporters of speciality cheeses.

The Acquisition of Ashley Chase Estate Limited

If you read the book "Ashley Chase – A Dorset Domain" by L.T.S. Littman, you will read the story of how Louis Littman started farming in Bride Valley, Dorset in 1965 and how he came to own a vast agricultural estate of dairy farms. Louis, a lawyer and property developer by profession, was never happier than when he was "living in the midst of one's fields and one's cattle, surrounded by one's family, one's work-people and their families and amidst all those who derive a livelihood from the land".

Louis Littman achieved much, but life can be cruel and in 1987, at the age of 62, he died of cancer leaving his widow Colette and sons Robbie and Cedric to mourn him. This was a tragedy for the family, Louis had still so much left unfinished. After his death Colette had major decisions to make and she was determined that these decisions would be according to what Louis would have wanted.

Robbie inherited the farm and Cedric inherited the cheese making dairy business. The milk from the farm was sold to the dairy and that is maintained today. Cedric's administrative skills ensured that the business would benefit from regional grants and his contacts in America created excellent exporting opportunities. When he met Mike Pullin he realised that Mike had experience, business acumen and was industrious, qualities which were needed to help him manage the business and Mike became a partner with a fifty percent shareholding.

In the years that followed it was not possible to maintain the estate according to Louis' original intentions and in 2010 a decision was taken to sell part of it. This included 108 acres of dairy farming land and the cheesemaking dairy. Consequently, following discussions with Cedric and Mike Pullin, Ashley Chase Estate Limited was purchased by Barbers and Mike Pullen joined the Board.

Ashley Chase make approximately 1200 tons of Cheddar annually and trade a further 1200 tons. Their Coastal mature cheddar cheese has been a very successful product and in 2012 it is probably the largest seller of English mature cheddar sold in the United States. Coastal has a sweet hint producing a calcium lactate crystal with a quite unique flavour. Cheese made at Ashley Chase is also marketed under the Ford Farm brand. The export arm is Ford Farm USA Llc based in New York and Seattle. "Cave Cheddar" made at Ashley Chase in Dorset but matured in Wookey Hole Caves in the Mendip Hills, is one of the largest selling Traditional Cylindrical mature cheddars sold in the United Kingdom.

Paul Nicholls

In the 1980's Manor Farm Racing Stables were created converting old barns and stables at Manor Farm where Paul lives and Jim Old rented the premises in the early years. When Jim Old left by mutual agreement, Paul Nicholls, an ex jockey who was keen to start his own National Hunt Racing Stable, approached Paul with a view to renting the facility.

On October 18th 1991 there began a long and very successful partnership as Paul Nicholls went from strength to strength and by 2012 he had achieved Champion National Hunt Trainer seven times. In two decades Paul Nicholls has developed a reputation for discovering and nurturing the best young equine talent into Champion Racehorses. Paul can claim to have the most powerful yard of National Hunt horses in the country.

Paul lives in the village with his family and the stables have brought much enjoyment and interest to local people. It is usual to see strings of horses winding their way through the village as they approach the Gallop. See More Business, Kauto Star, Master Minded, Big Buck's and Denman, to name but a few have all been hugely successful stars in the racing world.

In 1999 See More Business won the Gold Cup at the Cheltenham Festival - it completed Paul Barbers dream. He had passed the 1000 cow ownership many years earlier and Paul won the Gold Cup again in 2008 with Denman.

In April 2012 another dream was achieved, this time by Paul

Nicholls. On the first day of the Liverpool Festival he had a good start when Big Buck's (with Ruby Walsh on board) raced to a record 17th straight career win as he comfortably landed the World Hurdle at Aintree for the fourth consecutive year, the first horse to win this race four times. However, on the Saturday, 14th April, Paul won the Grand National with Neptune Collonges ridden by Daryl Jacob. It was the one accolade which had been missing from Paul's CV.

The next day over a thousand supporters and television crews were there to cheer Neptune Collonges and the team as they paraded through the village. This success sealed the race for the 2012 Champion National Hunt Trainer, Paul Nicholls had won it for the seventh time.

The Whey Processing Plant

In the 1990's a whey processing plant was installed. The main part of the process was ultra filtration which isolated and concentrated the whey protein to 50% solids. The remainder of the whey which consisted mainly of lactose was concentrated by reverse osmosis and sold to stock feeders. A useful bi-product from this process was warm soft water (30° C) which was used for cleaning purposes.

In 2005 the plant was expanded to include a drying facility in a joint venture with Carbery of Ireland. The newly formed company was named Barbery. Whey powder protein has many uses as an ingredient in health products, infant food, ice cream, etc. Much of this product is exported.

Starter Cultures

It is very important to mention the decision to establish a specialist Starter Culture Laboratory in the mid 1990's. This laboratory is dedicated to preserve and produce the natural mixed starter cultures historically used for making Farmhouse Cheddar. Generations ago these starter cultures were developed from the natural bacteria found in milk in the West Country and were exchanged between local cheesemakers. Over time, certain strains were found to make particularly good cheese and as technology moved on these have been isolated and refined.

Recent times have seen most cheesemakers move to use easier freeze dried or frozen "packet" starters which threatened the extinction of the traditional cultures. Ray Osborne a microbiologist with a long experience of cheese culture research and development joined the company in January 1997. He introduced improved methods for handling and storage of a collection of the cultures with the aid of Judith Rowsell who was appointed as his laboratory and production assistant. It took them five months to develop and write procedures, set up the new equipment and produce the seed cultures for the manufacture of the pints of starter cultures. The laboratory and production area was operational by June 1997.

Subsequent detailed studies of the cultures and their interactions made it possible to improve their stability and performance. An ongoing development program has enabled additional dependable cultures to be introduced to extend the range thereby ensuring that Barbers would be using this culture system for generations to come. The collection thrives today and although Barbers are the only Block Cheddar Farmhouse Cheesemakers who use these cultures, they are made available to many of the famous Traditional Cylindrical Farmhouse Cheesemakers. In 2009 Ray was awarded the MBE for services to the cheese industry.

Past, Present and Future

Three hundred years ago in 1712 John Barber was born. As a young man getting married at the age of twenty three he could not possibly have envisaged what future generations would achieve.

In 1851 John's great grandson Daniel Barber farmed 73 acres at Maryland Farm in Ditcheat, employing four Agricultural Labourers. In 2012 four of John Barber's sixth generation great-grand-sons, Chris, Charlie, Giles and Anthony are running the business with the support of a strong management team and have approximately 200 employees.

Although Paul has passed management of the land and farms to his son Chris, he has not retired and is never happier than when he is walking through the fields which generations of his family have walked. In the evening he enjoys checking on his National Hunt Racing horses in the stables close to Manor Farm where he lives. Those horses who have brought him much happiness and success when they were in their prime, are stabled close by or in summer will graze in the fields at Manor Farm.

Nicky too is now less involved in the business. He enjoys holidays and is still an enthusiastic sailor but on his return to Ditcheat will immediately wander down to the dairy to check up on the activities of the younger generation. In Paul and Nicky's life time the business has grown immensely. Throughout the years bold decisions have been made, long term relationships established and there has been much foresight from each generation.

In 2007 cheese production had risen to 7,000 tonnes. By 2012 the Barber Group turnover was approximately £65m, acreage 3200 and cattle stock 2000. Milk litreage produced on own farms approximately 14 million and milk litreage bought in from other West Country farms 95 million, to produce 13,000 tonnes of cheese per annum. The cold stores have been extended to a capacity of 13,000 tonnes and the building of new offices and laboratories were completed in the spring of 2012, officially opened by HRH The Countess of Wessex on the 21st of March.

Relationships with Supermarkets and other major customers remain strong and the export portfolio is expected to widen in 2013. The company continue to support the Trade and Cheese Shows and in 2011 at The World Cheese Awards Barbers won the *Best New Cheese Award* with their "1833" Vintage Reserve Cheddar and *Best Mature Cheddar Award* with their Mature Farmhouse Cheddar.

Generation after generation are aware that they are custodians for future generations. This is a story which really has no ending as the company goes from strength to strength.

It has been a privilege to have contributed to the story of this farming family.

(Author: Valerie Boothman - Joined 1972 – retired 2003)

Acknowledgements

Nicholas Barber

Paul Barber

Geoffrey Barber

Di Clements

Anna Giddings (nee Barber)

Gillian Cobden (nee Barber)

Patricia Savage-Bailey (nee Barber)

Chris Barber

Paul Nicholls

Peter Horner

Colette Littman

Mike Pullin

Ashley Chase – A Dorset Domain (LTS Littman)

Making Provision (Barty-King)

The Story of Fitch Lovell (Keevil)

Time Travellers Guide to Victorian Britain

The Society of Dairy Technology

And my family for their support and patience

The family line in Chronological Order

1712   John Barber born

1735   John Barber marries Joan Porch of West Pennard in Wells

1742   James Barber born in West Lydford – died 1808

1770   William Barber born – died 1842

1794   William married Elizabeth March in West Pennard

1809   William inherits much of his fathers estate – see will

1810   Daniel Barber born

1811   Daniel christened in Curry Rivel

1835   Daniel marries Rebecca Reakes in Ditcheat

1836   Alfred (son of Daniel) born in Ditcheat
        – later leaves for USA age 16

1842   Thomas (son of Daniel) born in Ditcheat

1843   Daniel inherits his father's estate

1852   Alfred leaves for America

1853   Daniel dies Maryland Farm Ditcheat

1867   (abt) Thomas Barber marries Emma Reakes

1868   William George (son of Thomas) born m Kate Emily Osborne

1870   Eliza Ellen (daughter) born m Ernest Henry Dyke in 1897

1872   Alfred Gerald (son of Thomas) born

1875   Daniel James (son of Thomas) born

1877   Elsie Lilian (daughter of Thomas) born m Leo Martin 1899

1880 Florence Rebecca (daughter of Thomas) born m Charles
Henry Butt

1897 Daniel James Barber died - committed suicide whist
depressed.

1900 Alfred Gerald m Mary Elizabeth Osborne of Chesterblade
age 19

1904 Mary Osborne (daughter of Alfred) born m George
Longman

1907 Thomas (son of Alfred) born – m Helen Look

1912 Alfred John (son of Alfred) born m Margery Weeks

1915 Reginald Gerald (son of Alfred) m Dorothy Steele Noel

1940 Patricia (daughter of Gerald) born
m Nigel Savage-Bailey

1941 Richard John Barber (son of Alfred John) born m
Margaret Urqhuart

1942 Paul Kelson Barber (son of Alfred John) born m Paula
Garrard Cole

1943 Thomas Nicholas Barber (son of Gerald) born m Diana
Walsh

1945 Anna (daughter of Alfred) born m John Giddings

1946 Gillian (daughter of Gerald) born m Richard Cobden

1966 Christopher (son of Paul) born m Emma Hillyer

1968 Giles (son of Paul) born m Jacqueline Robinson

1972 Charles (son of Nicholas) born m Helen Edgar

1974 Anthony (son of Nicholas) born

Census Records and Major Events in Chronological order

1841c Daniel living in Ditcheat with wife Rebecca

1851c Daniel and family living at Merry Lands

1871c Thomas aged 29 yrs living at Thorn Farm, North Barrow, Castle Cary

1881c Thomas aged 39 yrs living next to School Master House Ditcheat

1881c Wm George age 13 pupil at school in Wincanton High Street.

1891c Thomas aged 49 yrs living at Highbridge Farm Ditcheat also son Daniel aged 17

1891c William George (23) son of Thomas and older brother of Alfred Gerald, living with Sister Eliza Ellen (housekeeper age 20) at Rectory Farm – no others. Later Wm George marries and moves to Frome.

1897 Daniel James Barber living at Bengrove Farm

1901c Alfred Gerald aged 29 living at Rectory Farm Ditcheat

1901c Thomas aged 59 yrs living at Prospect House Ditcheat

1911c Thomas aged 69 yrs living at Prospect House

1911c Census shows Alfred Barber and wife and family living at Rectory Farm later known as Abbey Farm.

1920 Alfred Barber purchases 100 acres of land adjoining Maryland Farm from the Leir family at £100 per acre.

1930 Jack and Gerald Barber purchase Wards Farm

1939 Jack Barber buys Manor Farm Ditcheat

1952 Gerald Barber receives contract to make Caerphilly for South Wales

1955 Jack and Gerald negotiate a £100,000 loan with the bank to expand the business.

The business becomes a Limited Company.

1950/60's

The company exhibit at The Dairy Show at Olympia in London

1964 Meadow Milking Unit erected on land between Ditcheat and Alhampton already owned by the company

1966 Ringwell Milking Unit erected on the edge of Ditcheat on the Wraxall Road.

1967 Land purchased adjoining Dairy Farm House at Lower Wraxall and the farmhouse purchased. House sold to Frank Sutton. Years later re-purchased by the company.

1968 The land at Eastontrow purchased. Fields stocked and a new milking unit erected.

1972 The company purchased The Priory, Abbey Farm and sixty acres of land.

1972 First purpose built cold store built at Maryland Farm

1972 Packing plant facilities increased to accommodate cutting and packing for Rowson and Co of London.

1973 The company sold The Priory to Sir Christopher Chancellor.

1974 Purchase of land and farmhouse at Lower Wraxall.

1979 The land and farmhouse of Knowle Park, near Wincanton

was purchased.

1980 Cold storage capacity increased at Maryland Farm.

1981 Penn Barn Farm Dorset purchased (587 acres)

1984 Highbridge Farm purchased

1985 Barbers became members of The West of England and South Wales Provision Trade Association

1987 Site at Wiveliscombe near Taunton purchased and abattoir built for killing and curing pigs.

1989 The new "belt" system installed in the dairy

1989 Cold stores extended and packing plant built to house cutting and packing machinery purchased from J Sainsbury

1990 Block Cutter etc purchased from J Sainsbury

1990/1 Block formers introduced in the dairy.

1991 Paul Nicholls became a tenant of the National Hunt Racing Stables at Manor Farm Ditcheat.

1991 Company started selling to the Channel Islands

1992 Starter Culture Laboratory was built at Maryland Farm

1993 Whey Processing Plant was built.

1995 Abattoir sold

1998 Lower Sutton Farm purchased

1998 Barbers started exporting cheese to Spain

2002 Wincanton "tall towers" replaced Alpha Laval towers in the dairy

2003 Longwoods (Wraxall) purchased

2004 Wincanton vats were replaced by Tetra OST vats

2005 Whey Processing Plant expanded to include drying facility

2009 Company started exporting to the States through Somerdale International Ltd.

2010 The company acquired Ashley Chase Estate Ltd.

2012 Cold store extensions and new offices and Laboratories opened by HRH the Countess of Wessex.

Wills

The Last Will & Testament

Of James Barber (1742–1808) of West Pennard proven 1809

Executor Wᵐ William Barber

Power reserved to Betty Whittle wife of Jacob, and James Barber

Sum/property to :

daughter Alice Day £10

Grandson Benjamin Day...........£30 at 21 years old

Grandson John Higgins ....£30 at 21 years old

Brother James...........2 shillings per week for life unless able to work – then void

Son William Barber ....)

Daughter Betty Whittle ....) rest of the legacy

Grandson James Barber ....)

The Last Will & Testament

Of William Barber (1770-1842) of Ditcheat proven 1843

Executor James Barber (nephew) of West Lydford

And W.illiam Davis (Yeoman) of Doulting

Sum/property to :

Son Daniel Barber .... } All in trust

daughter Jane Barber ....)

daughter Jane Barber .... to be allowed to reside at the dwelling house in

.... Ditcheat

....

(At the time of his death only two of William's nine children survived him)

The Last Will & Testament

Of Thomas Barber (deceased 21st December 1916)
of Prospect House, Ditcheat, Somersetshire

Probate London 7th February 1917

Sum/property to :

Alfred Gerald Barber.............) Effects of £3361, 10 shillings and 6 pence
Charles Henry Butt (Yeoman).........)

The Barber Family Tree

(Male line summary)

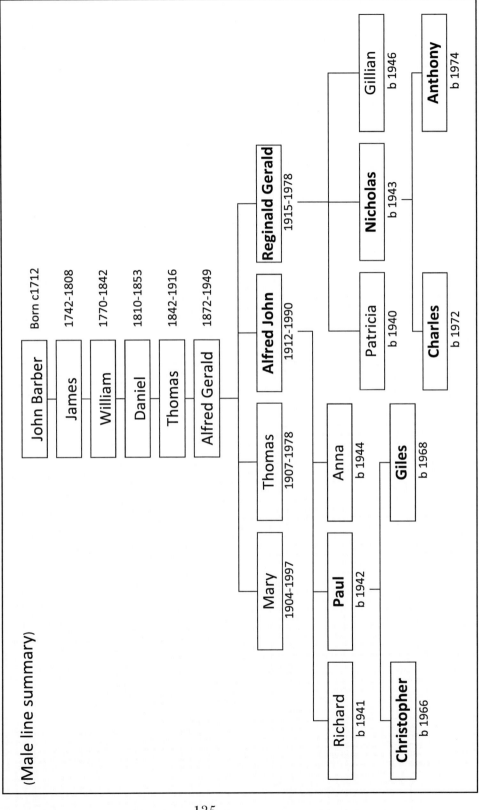

CERTIFIED COPY OF AN ENTRY OF DEATH

GIVEN AT THE GENERAL REGISTER OFFICE

Application Number 3760617-2

REGISTRATION DISTRICT SHEPTON MALLET

1916 DEATH in the Sub-district of Evercreech in the County of Somerset

Columns:—	1	2	3	4	5	6	7	8	9
No.	When and where died	Name and surname	Sex	Age	Occupation	Cause of death	Signature, description and residence of informant	When registered	Signature of registrar
276	Twenty first December 1916 Borynethaury Ditheat R.D.	Thomas Parfin	Male	74 years	Retired farmer	(1) Bronchia Pneumonia 4 days Certified by David Rice, M.B.	Alfred Gerald Parfin, Son, present at the death, Preston Farm Ditcheat	Twenty third December 1916	Herbert Liversidge, Registrar.

CERTIFIED to be a true copy of an entry in the certified copy of a Register of Deaths in the District above mentioned.

Given at the GENERAL REGISTER OFFICE, under the Seal of the said Office, the 13th day of January 2012

DYD 184754

CERTIFIED COPY OF AN ENTRY OF DEATH

GIVEN AT THE GENERAL REGISTER OFFICE

Application Number 3760617-1

REGISTRATION DISTRICT **SHEPTON MALLET**

1853 DEATH in the Sub-district of Evercreech in the County of Somerset

Columns:-	1	2	3	4	5	6	7	8	9
No.	When and where died	Name and surname	Sex	Age	Occupation	Cause of death	Signature, description and residence of informant	When registered	Signature of registrar
203	Twenty-Ninth May 1853 Pitchcott	Daniel Barber	Male	42 years	A Farmer	Consumption Not Certified	X The Mark of Ann Higgins Present at the Death. Kensington	Twenty-ninth May 1853	Joseph Williams Backhouse Registrar

CERTIFIED to be a true copy of an entry in the certified copy of a Register of Deaths in the District above mentioned.

Given at the GENERAL REGISTER OFFICE, under the Seal of the said Office, the 13th day of January 2012

DYD 184945

CERTIFIED COPY OF AN ENTRY OF DEATH

GIVEN AT THE GENERAL REGISTER OFFICE

Application Number 3760617-3

REGISTRATION DISTRICT   WELLS

1949   DEATH in the Sub-district of Shepton Mallet   in the   County of Somerset

Columns:-	1	2	3	4	5	6	7	8	9
No.	When and where died	Name and surname	Sex	Age	Occupation	Cause of death	Signature, description and residence of informant	When registered	Signature of registrar
353.	Sixteenth December, 1949. Park House, Ditcheat. R.D.	Alfred Gerald BARBER	Male	77 years	Farmer (retired)	1a. Cerebral Haemorrhage, b. Arterio Sclerosis, Certified by A.B.Liennie M.R.C.S.	Gerald Barber, Son, Present at the death Abbey Farm, Ditcheat.	Seventeenth December, 1949. 194	Clement W.Read. *Registrar*

CERTIFIED to be a true copy of an entry in the certified copy of a Register of Deaths in the District above mentioned.

Given at the GENERAL REGISTER OFFICE, under the Seal of the said Office, the   13th   day of   January   2012

DYD 184710

See note overleaf

JD

Photographs & Images

The photographs and images in this book have come from many different sources. Some from much thumbed albums, some from newspapers and some from the latest digital cameras. A decision has to be made on each photograph between quality and content. Where possible photographs have been enlarged to provide a better view of the subject matter and this may have resulted in a loss of quality or graininess that is unfortunately unavoidable. I hope this doesn't detract from your enjoyment of the book.